I0116899

Ours

Emily Skye

chipmunkapublishing
the mental health publisher

Published by
Chipmunkapublishing
United Kingdom

http://www.chipmunkapublishing.com

Copyright © 2014 Emily Skye

ISBN   978-1-78382-110-5

Mental health books give a voice to writers with mental health challenges around the world. At Chipmunkapublishing we raise awareness of mental health and the stigma surrounding mental health problems by encouraging society to listen. We are documenting mental health literature as a genre so history does not forget the survivors and carers of people with mental illness and disabilities.

Chipmunkapublishing gratefully acknowledge the support of Arts Council England.

For families everywhere and mine with love.

So that we find new ways together to speak the unspeakable
and bear knowing what is hard to be known.

Emily Skye

Contents

Introduction   9

Stone Heart   17

Ours Once More   19

Ours to Own   39

Heartstone   52

Emily Skye

Acknowledgements

Thank you Clare Kavanagh, Richard Morgan-Jones, Lally Freeborn and Tim Bramley. Without you, this would not have been possible.

Thank you to my poetry mentors Gillian Harries, Mary Meddings, Claire Williamson, and to Michele Findlay for the loving photography of my images.

Thank you for your depth of seeing enabling me to make this public Louise Partridge, Louise Knowles, Janet Woollard, Marion Taylor, Jill Hall, Mary Lynne Ellis, Noreen O'Connor, Isha McKenzie-Mavinga, Donald Findlater, Heather Townsend, Meg John Barker, Previn Karian, Miriam Taylor, Jen Pallet, Ruth Chipperfield, Caroline Lewis, Tricia Stewart, Abby Maitland, Jane Belshaw and dancers, Joan Simmons, Vienna Duff, Uschi Stickler, Marcia Worrell, Nadia Wager, Sussex Sisters and singers, Seaford Pride, Gestalt, Relational and OU communities. This is my gratitude expressed in one moment of time. If you think you might be included here you probably are, perhaps we have not yet even met.

Thank you to Chipmunkapublishers for being there so that 'Ours' can be spoken.

Thank you Sara, your love and steadfastness sustains me through the fear and joy of this book. You inspire me. Thank you to our beautiful Rocco. Thank you to my resilient, loving family. Most of all thank you to those who speak out with courage, and those who receive company and support from my book.

Emily Skye

Introduction

I will not impose meaning upon these poems or even a lens through which to read them. Meaning is a process, ever changing and my understanding of the messages in the poems continues to unfold. What they mean for you is yours. They arrived with me as offerings, bringing hope and clarity when I most needed this. I treasure them as mine, but they do not belong to me. I share them gladly in the hope that they gently accompany you along your way. I will tell you a little of my story, so that if you wish you can read this alongside the poems, not constraining or filtering their meaning for you, but simply offering some context of where they emerged in my life, which you can of course choose to read or not.

Part One

When I was three in the early 1970s, an older man befriended my young mother and stepfather. There had been disruption, sudden bereavement, historical trauma and divorce in our family as in many. Perhaps this vulnerability and family preoccupation added to our being sought out, perhaps not. This man told my parents fabricated stories of things they had in common and after a while offered to babysit, which as busy young parents, they gladly accepted. He continued to babysit for about five years during which time he sexually abused me. My parents saw my distress and responded, working hard to resolve things for me, even attending family therapy, but I had no way of articulating what was happening. I am not sure that I even knew what was happening, just that I was bad and felt horrible, distressed and angry. These feelings were understood in the context of the plausible other explanations, most centrally my parent's divorce.

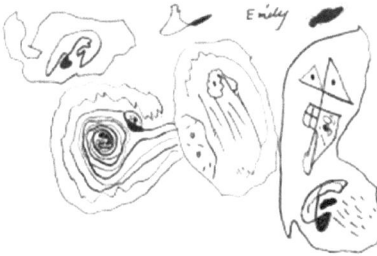

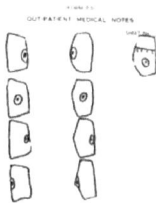

Emily   22 vii 79   Five months-

My
Name
is Hipp-
illMotic-
Tothano
FoLLcw-
OFell

OUT-PATIENT MEDICAL NOTES
SHEET No.

Twenty years later, studying to be a therapist and in therapy myself, I began to experience distressing symptoms in my body accompanied by feelings of overwhelm, panic and an increased awareness of holding on, holding in. I wrote 'Brace'. I wondered if these symptoms could be memories, but mainly dismissed this as a possibility. There was a lot of literature at the time about false memory syndrome. I worried that perhaps my symptoms were just associations from other people's stories about child sexual abuse. I began to ask more questions about my childhood. I had little memory of anything before the age of eleven and was beginning to realise this was unusual. My mother briefly mentioned the 'babysitter', but neither of us was able to grasp him as 'real' or 'knowable' at that time.

Ten years further on, a qualified, practising therapist, more memories emerged and the babysitter finally became 'real'. The story of meeting him in the park and even his name was possible to know and tell. The harm done to me was, by this time, more fully healing. I was becoming whole, reclaiming myself.

'Uncrushed' emerged suddenly, in a flood of words, one day, whole verses falling over one another to be placed on the page. During a busy day at work, I was finding two minutes here and there to capture this flood of words. At the end of that day, I managed to settle, to find the order of the verses, to see the whole that had been born.

'Uncrushed' was a gateway to a new life and a new way of becoming me in the world. I told the police everything I now knew about this man and I gave them my poem. They listened well and with deep respect, they heard my poem. They and I knew that it was almost impossible to find this man from what few details we had almost forty years later. Yet, they searched sincerely, and extraordinarily found him. Convicted of child sexual abuse in the 1990's, he had since died. Thankfully, the conviction happened before I had any inkling of the abuse, so that I could have not done more to protect others sooner. My family were able to identify him. The police took great care over my seeing his picture for the first time. The relief and resolution was immense. I wrote 'Welcome Home'.

Part Two

The following winter, the police arrested a loved and trusted member of my extended family for sexually abusing children. A tidal wave hit our family. Realities collided – what we knew to be true and what we now had to accept was true. I wrote 'Collisions'. Our whole family had welcomed this man. I had shared with him my recovery, my poems. I had 'seen' signs that I should have recognised, especially given my own experience and my professional knowledge, but somehow just as had happened several decades before, other explanations dominated. I did not let myself see or know. More than a year on, he pleaded guilty to all counts and is now serving his sentence. There are no maps for this, the right way to act. Pain dances around the family system, trying to find expression, someone to blame. 'Heart's Desire', 'First Stone', 'Freed' and 'Fault' carried me through this storm.

The inversion manifest in 'Stone Heart' to 'Heartstone' speaks of movement from stony silence, walled into the past to recognition of connecting hearts through time and space, guiding us with hope to the future, which is 'Ours'.

Emily Skye

Stone Heart

Like heart
        so ever stone
               reveals now
                    as then

as now reveals stone

                         ever so heart like

          heart so ever

                    stone reveals now

              as then as now reveals

stone ever

          so heart like

                 heart so ever stone

reveals now as then

Emily Skye

Ours Once More

Mother Love

Crippling pain of an unloved mother

battling to hold her children

giving from an empty cup

accused by all.

Twisted metal contortions

as she tries to mould herself into what she should yet be.

Harsh disjointed harmonies, too loud, ever present.

The glimmer of hope in a reaching glance met

raw shame unfolding.

At last, she sees

all see, that she is love

and this lens of love echoes back through

absence and pain of generations

giving thanks

and there is peace.

Brace

Hold on.

Tighten.

Keep in.

Keep out.

Restrict, breath, life, strength.

Keep upright, on guard, ready for anything.

Always prepared to end, never begin.

Stillness, paralysis, expression fixed, gives nothing away.

Jaw, throat tight. Dig, press, push in where energy stirs.

Do not feel, do not move, do not make a sound.

Deceive, whisper, weak, tired, helpless.

Give nothing. Take nothing. Risk nothing. Safe.

Dance of Silence

Beneath stone, of stone, in stone
stony stony silence, silenced
unturned
unknown.

Shouting, shouting
louder
louder
unseen.
Hush now.

Finally
finally speaking
listening
and sometimes
revealed by storm tides
upturned
known.

Emily Skye

A Love Song

Petals of fire

erupting in a stream of consciousness

facing in all directions

backwards beyond without within.

I do love you.

Storming ideas allowing revealed

uniting forces, power unleashed.

Will, want, won't, can.

Tenderly attending

graciously accepting

fondly remembering

rapidly unfolding

lovingly embracing

the many faces of me.

Uncrushed

You must have seen me that day in the park
through what distorted lens?
Inviting
You were not welcome
What did you say to charm your way in?

You stole my memories
replaced them with dark, hollow, echoes of a child lost and
afraid.

You are no longer part of me.

No.

***

Born too soon
a heart betrayed
fragility and weakness
you saw before you splayed.

Or perhaps it was my innocence
my life force or my joy
you couldn't see a person
an object, just a toy.

You didn't kill me then
you have not killed me now.
I wasn't yours to take
that wrong I won't allow.

Indeed, you had an impact
delayed me and dispersed
but now I'm coming together
we've freed me from your curse.

Now I choose my rhythm
you don't get to play my tune
from minor key to major key
a symphony abloom.

Yes, let me tell you something, you and all your kind
for every child who suffers you I hope I change your mind.
For every ounce of venom you poured into my soul
the antidote was stronger and it's nearly made me whole.

The ice that once enveloped me
now fire within my depths.
That little girl you stole from
is taking her own steps.

My limbs are now unfurling
blood coursing through my veins
my sexual self is mine now
no longer in such pain.

Contortions are not needed
distortion, so much less.
Limit to my potential
is anybody's guess.

***

To all of you abusers
I want to say just this.
The antidote is plentiful
facing the abyss.

If you have the courage
there could be some for you.
It hurts to deep dive through your soul
but then you could renew.

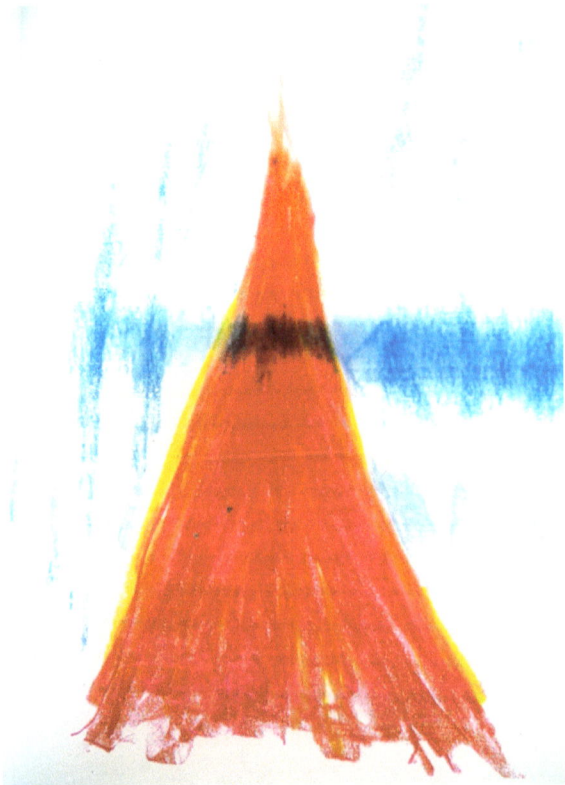

My Mother Wept

One night in 1974,
        two little girls were left in your care.
She couldn't know, didn't know
        how disturbed you were
But somewhere deep inside
        beyond the conscious mind
she knew

and my mother wept.

She wept for all the pain, loss, betrayal and shame.
She wept for what had already happened
relentlessly in humankind.
Over and over and over again.

Wishing Well, Well-Spring

Echoes pool endlessly backwards
whispers just out of reach
shadowy distractions from now
yet substantial enough to well
walling out the future
walling in the past.

But beneath the waves
deep beneath the waves
lies God's honest truth
simple timeless truth
that we are free.

Dawn

The threads of the web make themselves known
infinite
astonishing
beautiful.

New dew shimmering, quivering in the light
strong, fragile across time and space
everything intimately connected
in love.

Alight

A roaring fireball rolls around the world
darkness closes in
suffocating the light
completely.

But there is still light
shards of light shining from every being
beaming, bellowing light
peeling back the darkness
revealing the fire belly of the earth
alive alight.

Aligned

As I align with my will
becoming who I am
no longer matters.

Yet who I am is clearer
each moment
each meeting

selfing, transforming
beyond and beyond and beyond.

From here
I receive
believe
take a stand
know how to act.

I will
wholly aligned with myself
knowing my surrendered self.

Meeting, selfing, transforming

beyond

beyond

beyond.

Ours

Welcome Home

Welcome home little one
I know you
you belong with me.

Ours to Own

Collisions

Everything still
suspended momentarily
gazing upon itself.
Even the rain
drizzles unobtrusively.

My ghost feet tread
echoing the glazed sea
the hushed wind
your quietly dancing paws.

Timeless shelter from
stop-dead collisions
creating a void between
before and now
more than a lifetime
less than an in-breath.

In the between time
when we are still of the scene
nothing makes sense.
Later, we will see
with the gentle gaze of time itself
just what comes to pass.

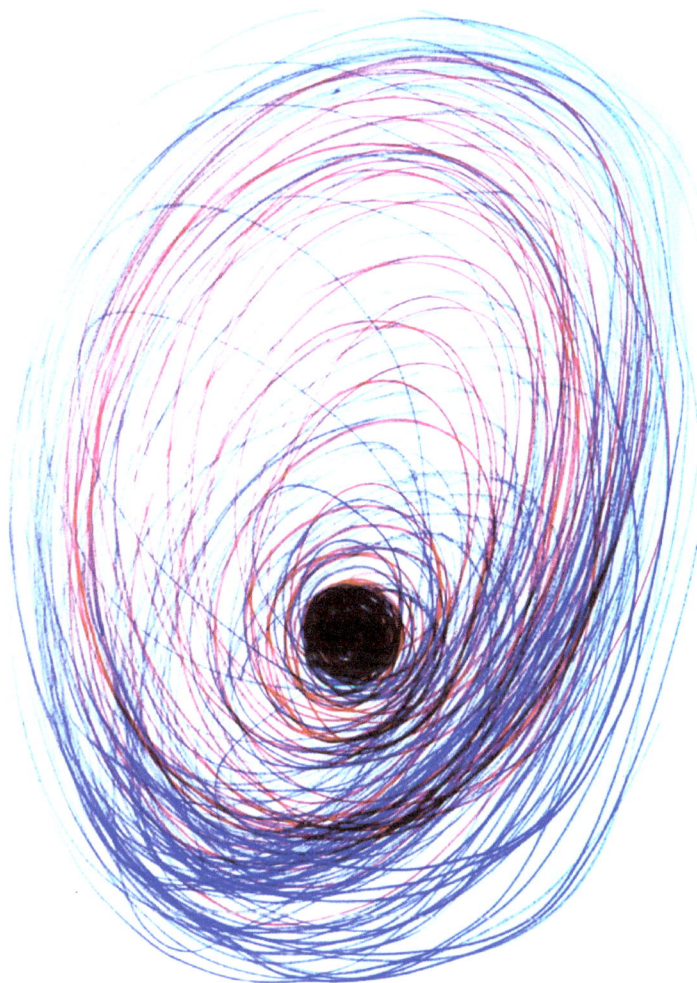

Heart's Desire

Free to love to move to become.

Not our family loyalty to itself

unseeing fear that rips

ripples endlessly on

so that another child

soul and body

is taken and twisted

to feed the dragon

who is ours

to know

to own.

First Stone

You didn't see
that 'surprises' me.

I accuse me
you accuse you
I accuse you
you accuse me.

Horrified
shocked
appalled
by you.

I accuse me
you accuse you
I accuse you
you accuse me.

I excuse me
you excuse you
I excuse you
you excuse me.

Freed

Freed from lies
guilty plea releases
stopping
finally stopping
and knowing
and knowing
and knowing
what I did to you
and do no more.

Fault

The night I ended the world
I died and woke up peaceful.

Purposefully
mightily
shifted the plate

then I knew.

The fault zone first
almost silent

whose fault

just fault.

After the still
inevitable, compelled
the land gave way.

Chasms, tremendous swathes
falling, folding in
Unfathomable sound
feel the falling beneath
foundations
all gone
falling, folded into earth
subsumed, embraced, consumed

I died and woke up peaceful
the night I ended the world.

Ours

Untitled

Her soul spoke to mine
so the final thread was sewn
your sparkle woven too
and my first born.

Never again
let them
reduce you.

Instead hear.

No. Stop, wait.Hear.

Each

every

word

yours

mine

unspoken

sung

The well-battered wall gone
illusion all along
and you
beautiful mammalian bird
soar on.

Ours

Lasting Impressions

I imagine as our life draws in,
a space opens up within each moment
I wonder whether that space
fills with impressions
first impressions
lasting impressions
of what and who impressed
pressed on us.

and what of the lasting impressions we leave
our well-trodden footpaths
guiding others through fields
to share in the landscape
through the same rough ground
that tripped us up
and those before us.

Our recipes folded into the family fabric.
How to bake a cake.
How to build a home.
How to cherish a loved one.
How to survive a tragedy.

I hope that from the space between the moments
erupts molten liquid light
pouring relentlessly into the caves of our being
until there is no part of us
left empty and untouched.

I pray that this brings deep peace.
I wonder if these impressions
dance themselves into a tapestry
a perplexing work of art
received wholly as our own
and at the same time our unique offering.

Heartstone

Everstone reveals

now as then as now

heart like heart

ever so.

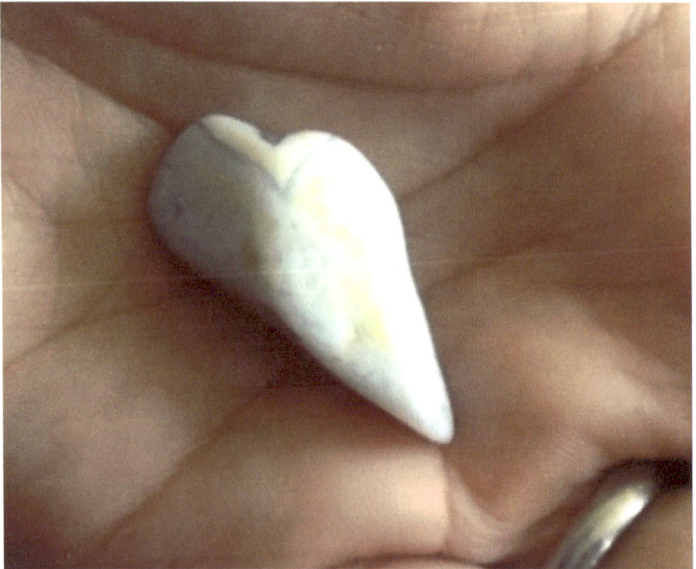